C000224884

# Sacred Spa

## a Spiritual Guide to Nurture
## Your Inner Power

## by Phoebe Garnsworthy

**Also By Phoebe Garnsworthy:**
Lost Nowhere: A Journey of Self-Discovery (Vol. 1)
Lost Now Here: The Road to Healing (Vol. 2)
Daily Rituals: Positive Affirmations to Attract Love,
Happiness, and Peace
The Spirit Guides: A Short Novella
Define Me Divine Me: a Poetic Display of Affection
And still, the Lotus Flower Blooms

Sacred Space Rituals: a Spiritual Guide to Nurture Your Inner Power
ISBN: 978-0-6488396-2-0
Copyright © 2020 by **Phoebe Garnsworthy**
**Cover Artwork by Andrea Hrnjak**
All rights reserved. No part of this publication may be reproduced,

distributed or transmitted in any form or by any means, without prior

written permission.

www.PhoebeGarnsworthy.com

# Contents

# Introduction

Welcome to your Sacred Space Rituals, your spiritual guide to nurture and protect your inner power.

Enclosed within these pages are spiritual tools, techniques and practices that aim to align you with your Higher Self.

These pages have been created by calling upon ancient spiritual philosophy from around the world. They primarily use the principals of creative visualization while harnessing the abundance of universal energies that surround you. The purpose of this book is to assist you on your journey of personal development and spiritual transformation.

You are the wisest healer you could ever ask for, and all the answers you seek are within. Call upon these practices to ignite the power of your soul as you journey through life and conquer your quest for greater fulfillment. We begin by learning how to set up your sacred space ritual, and from here, you will learn various tools and techniques to harness the power of the Universe around you. Under each ritual you will be given a few journaling questions to help ignite the changes that you seek.

# Creating Your Sacred Space Ritual

**Balance Your Mind, Body + Soul**
Ground Yourself & Calm Your Mind with Slow Deep Breaths

**Set Your Intention**
Speak it Out Loud & Write it Down

**Ask For Guidance**
"I call upon Spirit to Honor this Space
with Your Love and Blessings"

**Ignite Your Sacred Space**
Assemble, Touch and Talk to your Symbols that represent
the Universal Energies: Earth, Air, Fire, Water, Spirit.

**Meditate + Envision**
Close your eyes and imagine the feeling of your intention
coming into fruition. Allow your energy to vibrate at this
high frequency as you release any part of yourself that is
holding you back from fulfilling your life purpose.

**Give Gratitude + Close the Circle**
Thank Spirit and the Universal Energies for their blessings.

*Phoebe Garnsworthy*

# Creating Your Sacred Ritual

Creating rituals are an important tool to support our ultimate goals. When we speak our intentions to the Universe, we are co-creating our future, and when we compliment this practice with a ritual, our manifestations elevate and escalate into fruition.

To create your ritual you need to do three things;
**One** - define your space, which you can achieve through creating a sacred altar.
**Two**, state your intention (speaking out loud, writing it down, or visualizing the outcome you desire).
And **three**, invite spirit in to support your desires. When these three aspects are combined, you have successfully created your own sacred ritual.

To create your sacred altar and define your space, gather something tangible to represent the following elements - earth, air, water, fire and spirit. You can add more than 5 pieces, but this is the minimum amount needed to harness the universal energies. Suggestions as follows:

**Earth** is connected to nature and provides grounding, security and harvesting. Symbols for Earth could be a crystal, a rock, a plant or a bowl of dirt.

**Water** represents our emotional wellbeing. It is used for reflection, healing and nurturing. Symbols for water could be a shell, a small glass of water or a jar of salt.

**Air** signifies knowledge, courage, clarity and detachment. Symbols for air could be some incense, a feather or essential oils.

**Fire** initiates creative and sexual energy, strength and protection. Symbols for fire could be a candle, an obsidian crystal, a piece of wood or an item that represents the color red.

**Spirit** praises our Eternal Self, our Soul, the Source of Life Force Energy. Choose something to represent yourself, an idea of this could be - a photo of yourself, a figurine of any kind, or a drawing you created.

Set up your sacred altar by placing your items in a way that feels beautiful to you. As you commence your ritual allow yourself the freedom to be drawn to the elements in whatever way you wish, there is no right or wrong way to do this. Trust the power within your heart, and allow spirit to guide you.

Once you have created a space that you feel comfortable with, set your intention. That is - what is the reason for this ritual? What do you hope to achieve from calling upon the powerful spirits of the Universe?

Examples:
"I am igniting this ritual to . . . . "

"I call upon the energy of the Universe to support my vision of . . . "

Take a few deep breaths, calling upon each energy for its blessing and guidance. Keep your journal and pen next to your altar so that you may write down your manifestations and any messages that come through to you in this sacred space.

The purpose of your sacred altar is to honor your soul with self-love and self-care. As you cultivate this energy in your sacred space, you will in return bring forth a deeper connection between you and your soul.

*Journaling Questions:*
*When calling in spirit, do I have any ancestors, or someone who has passed over who I could call upon?*
*Where in my house, or garden could I create a sacred space to ignite my rituals?*
*What items do I already have that represent each of these elements?*

# Morning and Evening Rituals

Our habits are the driving force that guide us to creating the change that we seek. In order to achieve our goals we must start with small changes everyday. Ask yourself: What is it that I am seeking today?

Then write down what actionable steps you can take or are currently taking to support this goal. But the main question is - how often are you doing them? Repetition of our habits will bring us the results that we are seeking. The only person who is responsible for change in your life is yourself.

By creating small positive changes in our daily routine we are contributing to our own personal development, raising our vibration higher and shifting our consciousness to lead a fulfilled life.

On the following pages are my favorite morning and evening rituals that I use to channel my inner power.

As you look over these pages, notice how I incorporate the universal energies that you have used previously when creating your sacred altar.

This is how we embody and harness the universal energies around us, by weaving them into our daily routine and interacting with them as often as possible.

The universal energies of earth, air, fire, water and spirit are available to you in abundance and for free! When you combine this knowledge with awareness as you connect with the life force energies around you, you will effortlessly unite your mind, body and soul in a harmonic balance. We can tap into the abundance of spiritual wisdom that surrounds you through connecting with these energetic elements often.

The more you practice and tune into the messages from these gatekeepers of wisdom, the more spiritually enlightened you will become.

Of the list below, pick at least one to do each morning and evening, and slowly, bit by bit, add to it. Take what works for you and discard the rest.

*Journaling Questions:*
*Do I feel more energetic in the morning or evening?*
*At what point of time in my day do I need help creating more peace? What is something I already do in the morning or evening that makes me feel good?*
*How can I include this into my list of morning or evening rituals?*

# Morning Rituals:

**Cleanse + Refresh**
Drink Fresh Water & have a Shower

**Attract Abundance**
Write down 3 things you are Grateful for

**Connect Mindfully**
Inhale + Exhale Five Deep Breaths

**Ignite Clarity + Creativity**
Burn Candles, Incense or Oils

**Self-Heal**
Meditate for 10-30 minutes

**Be Open to Change**
Stretch Your Body with Yoga or Dance

**Manifestation**
Write down Your Goals / Intentions for the Day

**Nurture with Self-Love**
Go for a Walk in Nature

*Phoebe Garnsworthy*

# Evening Rituals:

**Invite Peace**
Relax Your Body in a Warm Bath

**Encourage Self-Love**
Write down 3 things you did well Today

**Release Stagnant Energy**
Stretch or Self-Massage

**Harmonize Your Soul**
Breathe In & Out Deeply x 5 times

**Welcome Clarity + Lightness of Being**
Meditate for 10-30 Minutes

**Self-Soothe**
Drink a Hot Tea, or Smell Essential Oils

**Attract Success**
Envision the Life You want to Live

**Rest + Replenish**
Ask for Protection as you Dream

*Phoebe Garnsworthy*

# Breathing Meditation

### Breathe In:
I am Safe, I am Loved, I am at Peace

### Breathe Out:
I release anything that no longer serves me

### Breathe In:
I receive healing, nourishing and loving energy

### Breathe Out:
I release my fears, my worries, my stress

### Breathe In:
I am Safe, I am Loved, I am at Peace.

Phoebe Garnsworthy

# Breathing Meditation

If you are looking to make one change in your life, let it be this: learn how to use to your breath to harmonize the flow of energy between your mind, body and soul. This is achieved by taking deep inhalations and exhalations, very slowly.

Our breath is the most powerful tool we own.
It opens the gateway to the realm of unconsciousness and in this space we can tap into the infinite wisdom that surrounds us. When we do this, we self-soothe and bring our awareness into the present moment, thus creating peace and balance into our life.

Using our breath we are able to seek refuge within our own body, uniting our spiritual self and our human existence together in our sacred space. This grounds our soul into reality, bringing forth confidence and clarity to our life.

Once you learn how to harness the power of your breath through meditation, you will enter a state of utter bliss upon the first moment of closing your eyes.
The more you consistently practice meditation, the greater rewards you will reap.

When we open the pathway to the guidance of our soul we are able to journey through life with profound wisdom and understanding, providing us the strength and power to handle any challenge that comes our way.

And all of this can be achieved from the simplicity of just our breath!

To harness this feeling of pure love in your life, repeat the spiritual blessing on the page prior while in a sacred space on your own. Breathe in and out very slowly and read the words with each motion of inhalation and exhalation.

Once you are in a deep state of relaxation, recite your favorite mantra or self-love affirmation to engrave this message upon your heart. Or if you wish to speak with spirit to learn the advice you need to hear this day, now is your time to do so. Try to repeat this breathing exercise every day and notice how different you feel before and after.

*Journaling Question:*
*Breathe in and out slowly (counting to 5), and repeat the affirmations above x 5 times.*
*After doing so write down how you feel.*
*Do you feel relaxed? At peace? Calm?*

# To My Higher Self

Your Higher Self is your soul, in the unseen worlds, who is watching you live your life out in reality. It is you in the most purest loving light energetic form. Your soul in the spirit realm is connected to the abundance of love and infinite wisdom, and in this space, you have complete clarity over your life, bringing forth the understanding of who you are and why you are here. But when your soul journeys through the unseen worlds from your 'Higher Self' and into your physical body, you disconnect from the abundance of enlightened energy that surrounds you, forgetting the truth of your divine self. This disconnection enables you to experience a life on Earth in human form. This is so you learn how to evolve consciously enabling you to fulfill your soul contract.

Your soul contract is a series of life lessons and challenges that are predestined in order for you to derive great meaning from your life and support your ascension to the new plane of existence. Although your soul contract may feel difficult at times, it is exactly what you need.

We spend a lot of time learning how to navigate our lives, seeking support on how to create the most valuable experiences that will provide us peace, love and happiness. We think that it is difficult but in fact, once we learn how to tap into the infinite wisdom of the Universe by connecting with our Higher Self we learn how easy and pleasurable life can really be.

Using spiritual tools and techniques such as journaling, meditations and rituals, you are able to connect with your Higher Self and call upon the infinite wisdom that surrounds you.

To do so, have a clear idea of the questions you need help with, ignite your sacred space and call in spirit using your Higher Self Blessing. To channel your Higher Self, begin by entering a deep state of meditation and envision your Higher Self. View this beautiful version of yourself in the purest form and speak confidently to it. Trust is the key in this moment, for you need to hold faith that the right answers are being delivered to you. Practice often and know that your Higher Self is divinely guiding you at all times.

*Journaling Questions:*
*What does my higher self look like?*
*What does the energy of my Higher Self feel like?*
*Find something in your room that can be a tangible representation of your Higher Self. Hold this item and set your intention to place the energy of your Higher Self inside it. Whenever you need extra strength, call upon this power object.*

# To My Higher Self:

I am ready to receive the abundance

of blessings that are waiting for me.

And with your support by my side, I manifest my goals,

my dreams and my visions into fruition.

With an open heart I speak with clarity.

And I honor my space, my peace and divinity.

I move in alignment with the harmonious vibrations of the Universe.

With you by my side, I can accomplish anything I set my mind to.

And I know you are with me always.

And so I thank you.

*Phoebe Garnsworthy*

# Ritual to Listen to Your Intuition

Calm your mind with 5 x deep breaths
and place your hand on your heart.
Envision a question, write it down
and be open to feeling the truth.
Recite the following words:


I am not alone, I feel you here with me
and together, we are weaving the journey of my life.
Every breath brings me closer to you,
as the stillness in my mind opens our channel of communication.
I hear you voice clearly as you guide me on this pathway.
Supported, nurtured and safe, I feel your love, I feel your grace
and I open myself to receive your divine message on this beautiful day.


Take note of any thought or message that comes to mind
and give gratitude for the wisdom from your Higher Self.


Phoebe Garnsworthy

# Ritual to Listen to
# Your Intuition

Your intuition is the communication channel between your Higher Self (your soul in the unseen worlds) and your reality. It is a cord of energy light that provides you with feelings, words and definite knowings about people, places and situations. You receive these messages through your intuition, directly from your Higher Self.

The more we strengthen our intuition, the clearer these messages will become. To strengthen our intuition channel we turn to meditation and journaling.

Meditation clears the communication pathway of your intuition, removing any negative thoughts or stagnant energy that is holding you back from hearing the true wisdom to navigate your life path. When we combine meditation with journaling we can document any advice from our Higher Self easily, enabling clarity and understanding through its messages.

The more you practice listening, learning and trusting your intuition, the easier it will become to distinguish the voice between what is real and what is not.

Find a space where you can be alone, get a journal and pen and follow the ritual on the page prior. Once you have connected with your intuition, practice with the following exercise.

Write down any question or problem that you need help on and then answer the question without thinking about it. This enables a moment of truth to be spoken before your mind tries to take control.

Remember - you hold the greatest wisdom you could ever seek. Don't ever forget it!

*Journaling Questions:*
*Imagine the communication line of your intuition to your Higher Self.*
*What does my intuition channel look like (color, texture)?*
*What can I do to help strengthen my intuition?*
*What activities make me feel closer to myself and provide me with confidence?*
*If I needed one question answered by my intuition today, what would it be?*

# Energy Protection Meditation

At the core of every living thing is vibrating energy. At every moment of every day we are giving and receiving energy. When we radiate loving vibrations, we in turn receive those loving vibrations. And likewise, if we emit negative energy, we will attract that same energy. But sometimes, when we are giving positive vibrations, it is attractive to all levels of energy, and often, other people can drain you of this energy unknowingly, as well as dark energy sticking to you. It is for this reason that we need to recite an energy protection meditation to seal our own divine power and ensure others hold their energy too.

To begin, tune into the energy around you by taking note of how you feel as you move through your life. When you interact with another person do you feel good or exhausted? When entering spaces of nature or people's homes do you feel uplifted or irritated?

The more we become aware of how energy affects us, the easier it will be to protect our energy, cleanse our energy and rejuvenate our soul, thus providing ourselves with the most optimal environment to live our life.

Use this energy protection meditation at any time throughout the day. To first initialize it, do so in a mediative state, but once this has been created, you can envision this energy protective bubble at any time of any day from there on out. Even with your eyes open! When imaging the bubble of light energy surrounding you, envision this bubble to reach as open as an arms width (this is the size of your aura).

This energy protection meditation will protect your energy from absorbing negative vibrations, and prevent energy leakage. It is also a useful tool for protection while sleeping to prevent nightmares. You can envision this protective bubble around your children, loved ones and even your house. This is your sacred space and everyone deserves their own sacred space. This bubble of protection encourages each and every one of us to stand strong within our own power.

*Journaling Questions:*
*Is there anyone in my life who drains my energy?*
*What places in nature do I feel the most energetic?*
*What activities makes me feel empowered?*
*What's my favorite way to cleanse and recharge my energy?*
*How often am I doing these things?*

# Energy Protection Meditation

Close your eyes and take 3 deep breaths in and out.
Imagine a white light from above streaming down upon
you like a waterfall.
This light is pure, loving energy.
The light flows around you completely,
and circles you like a giant bubble.
This bubble of light is your sacred space.
You are safe here.
Nothing can harm you, nor come into your energy field.
Envision this bubble solidifying and say out loud:
"I command my sacred space."
This light is here to protect your energy.

*Phoebe Garnsworthy*

# Affirmations to Calm Anxiety, Stress and Fear

At some point in our lives we are confronted with the challenge of learning how to nurture our mental well-being. These challenges most likely will come in the form of anxiety, depression, stress or fear and make us feel as though we have no control over ourselves or our life. But this is simply not true. Because you always have control over your breath, and you can use this to anchor your soul into your body to self-soothe as you overcome any feelings of unease. But before you do this, it's important to learn what it is that you're going through in order to focus on prevention and to identify the symptoms when they arise.

To recognize your mental health symptoms, take note of the emotions you are feeling. These emotions will relate to either anxiety or depression. From here, learn the best tools and techniques you can to self-soothe and prevent it from reoccurring. All mental health issues are a request from within to make a change in your life. There is something you need to reveal in order to heal, the question is - what is it?
You hold the answer to this question, but when you ask your intuition what it is, you must be prepared to accept what is spoken.

Open yourself up to the wisdom of the cosmos through channeling your Higher Self and journal through the following questions:
Where does this pain come from? What is this anxiety / stress / fear here to teach me? Know that these emotions and feelings are not here to stay, you can overcome them, but to do so, you must first, accept that they are there.

The following breathing exercises and affirmations on the next pages are some suggested ways to calm yourself when feeling the symptoms of mental health surfacing and are also useful for preventative measures.

By using the tools of your internal breath and reciting positive affirmations you will shift the negative energy from within, allowing new vibrations to take its place.

*Journaling Questions:*
*Tune into the energy of your body, ask yourself -*
*How do I feel about my mental and physical health right now?*
*What can I do to support my mental and physical health?*
*If you feel any symptoms, write down what they are and explore the possible reasons why.*
*From here, create a plan for how to nurture and heal yourself.*
*Stick to that plan consistently (daily)!*

# Peace. Tranquil. Calm.

You have control over your mind and your body.

You can calm yourself with your breath.

Do this by exhaling longer than inhaling.

Inhale for 1, 2, 3, 4.

Exhale for 1, 2, 3, 4, 5.

Repeat this until you feel your presence calm down.

Ground your soul into your body with the help of your crystals.

Calm your mind with the soothing scent of Mother Nature.

Invite mindfulness into your space as you light your candle and focus on the flame.

Relax and self-soothe with a heart-nourishing bath.

*Phoebe Garnsworthy*

With every breath I become more relaxed and at peace.

The emotions I feel do not define me, they are simply visitors.

I have the ability to solve any problems that cross my path.

I release negative thoughts and welcome positive vibrations.

I have control over my breath, my mind, my body and my life.

I am doing the best I know how to.

I am talented, beautiful and intelligent.

I have a unique gift to give the world.

I am a magnet for success.

*Phoebe Garnsworthy*

# Calming Affirmations
# for Depression

You are so much more than your thoughts and emotions. You are vibrating energy that circulates, refreshes and renews. Whenever we are feeling stuck in our skin, it's important to release and rejuvenate our energy from within.

Depression can be the feeling of our soul floating above our body. It's not in our Higher Self, nor in reality, it's stuck somewhere in between. In order to call back our soul we need to accept where we are in this moment, for resisting life only leads to pain. To do so, we want to create a safe haven for our soul to return to and we do this by cleansing our own energy and inviting in new harmonious vibrations to take its place. This is achieved by turning to the natural resources around you of earth, air, water and fire. Experiment with each element and take note of what works best.

Air - is going for a long walk outside and allowing the fresh breath of life energy to circulate and renew your energetic being.

Earth is getting your hands dirty in the ground through gardening or meditating and connecting with the energetic gravity that pulls you below.

Water is swimming in the ocean, a bath or shower and letting the water soothe your emotions and cleanse your vibrations.

Fire is releasing your troubles to the flame of a candle or a bonfire and allowing the energy to transform and refresh.

Other ideas to self-soothe involve creativity such as singing, dancing, drawing and exercise. Anything that helps release energy so that it can transform into something else. But not always do we feel like doing something. And that's okay too. Whenever you are feeling uncertain, or a bit lost, use your breath to calm your soul and read over the affirmations to remind yourself that these emotions won't last.

Everything changes and life is full of highs and lows.

*Journaling Questions:*
*What element makes my mind feel at peace and cleansed?*
*Earth, water, fire or air? (It can be more than one).*
*How often am I connecting with this energy and cleansing my own vibration?*
*At what point in my life did I feel most in control and empowered? What was I doing?*

# Remember

This emotion that you feel is only temporary.

You will feel yourself again.

You will be braver and stronger than you ever were before.

You are never alone.

The Universe is vibrating within you.

You are full of miracles, of magic.

You have endless beauty within your heart.

You have control over your life.

Take a deep breath, place your hand over your heart

and come home to yourself.

*Phoebe Garnsworthy*

With every breath I nurture love throughout my body

and with every exhale I release fear, worry and stress.

I surrender into the present moment knowing
that my life is unfolding as it is meant to.

I give myself permission to enter this stage of
uncertainty with grace and elegance.

I welcome challenges with an open heart and a curious mind.

I have the strength to handle anything that comes my way.

I release the past knowing that I did the best that I could.

I let go of regret and create space for new beginnings.

I have everything that I need right now.

I am always enough.

*Phoebe Garnsworthy*

# Setting Boundaries

Boundaries can be defined as the standard of behavior and code of ethics that you deem appropriate from other people and also yourself.

Setting boundaries is an important act of self-love. It determines your relationships with yourself, others and also in the workplace.

If we do not establish and communicate our boundaries clearly, it emits the impression that we don't respect ourselves and in turn, gives people permission to take advantage of us. When we create boundaries we are honoring ourselves. When we communicate our boundaries we are teaching other people the level of love and respect that we deserve, because we are setting the example to ourselves first.

Boundaries also protect your energy and ensure that you are putting your needs first, because it is only from this place that you can give others equal respect and love. Learning what boundaries work for you is life changing!

Open your journal and begin brainstorming a list of boundaries that are relevant to you in this moment of time. Refer to the list on the following page to help you with this.

And then, reflect over your life to troubling events that you have faced where you wish you had acted differently.

Ask yourself, "If I had created a boundary, would I still feel this way?"
Regret is never a bad thing, because through this we are able to grow into better versions of ourselves. The best way to evolve is through facing difficult challenges and self-reflecting our actions and experiences.

Now, examine the challenge and recall as to whether the person involved acted in a way that made you feel uncomfortable, or if their words did not align with your values, your beliefs and perhaps it even insulted your self-love or self-respect. This is an opportunity to establish and communicate a boundary to stop that behavior from continuing.

Establishing our boundaries is the first step, and communicating them, is the second. We need to be transparent with our intentions and open communication so that others can also evolve into better versions of themselves. We are constantly a mirror to one another, providing gateways of growth and understanding, compassion and love to blossom within our conscious minds.

It's important to stand strong by your boundaries, despite another persons opinion. You must also agree that everyone also deserves the same respect and equal right to their own boundaries. We are all different, and just because we think differently doesn't mean that one person is superior to another. But, the more we voice our needs and wants with love and truth, the more we will find the right people who agree and support our ideas, thus creating a strong and unbreakable bond of trust in our circle of friends.

*Journaling Questions:*
*What boundaries are important to me?*
*What behavior do I find acceptable?*
*What areas of my life feel unbalanced?*
*Can I create a boundary to support strengthening and balancing this area of my life?*
*Are there any problems that arise continuously that need to stop? How can I create a boundary to support breaking this cycle?*

# Setting Boundaries:

- It's okay to say no

- Nobody has to agree with me

- I have a right to feel safe and respected

- I am responsible for my own happiness

- It's not my responsibility to make others happy

- I have the freedom to choose my lifestyle choices

- I'm allowed to express my opinions, needs and feelings

- I give myself permission to be who I am without apologizing

- I am enough exactly as I am, right in this moment

*Phoebe Garnsworthy*

# I Give Myself Permission

What do you give yourself permission for today? So often we get caught up in what we think we should be doing or feeling. But the moment we surrender and accept ourselves in the present moment is when we finally find the peace we are seeking.

Take a moment to feel the truth within your heart and release the words your soul desires. This is your life, your world, your destiny. Give yourself permission to be you.

You get to choose what vibrational frequency you wish to reside in. There's no right or wrong choice. What you want may not necessarily be the same for another. And that's okay. We are all living according to our own level of awareness. What we should all be doing and wanting for each other is to live in alignment with our Higher Self and be the greatest version of ourselves.

*Journaling Questions:*
*What do I give myself permission for today?*
*What can I do (activity) to support my answer above?*
*Look at the list, write down an activity that supports each point.*

# I give myself permission:

to rest
to heal
to be me
to say no
to change
to love myself
to ask for help
to make mistakes
to pursue my dreams
to live, play, laugh and dream

*Phoebe Garnsworthy*

# New Moon Prayer

The new moon signals that it's a time for new beginnings! The absence of moonlight ignites a moment for self-reflection, for it is a blank canvas to birth new ideas and sew the seeds of manifestations. The question is - what do you want to achieve in this moon cycle?

Use the energy of the new moon to tap into the unlimited abundance and call in what it is that you wish to manifest through the month ahead.

Do this by first opening up your sacred space and harnessing the energy that surrounds you. In this time we can also call upon the spiritual energy of Grandfather Sun and Grandmother Moon and invite them in to bless our space.

*Journaling Questions:*
Open up your journal, write down the day's date and commence your manifestations.

*What do I want to manifest this new moon?*
*What do I want more than anything right now?*

If you have a few things, that's great! Make a list of your greatest desires, and callings from your soul. Aim high! There is nothing that you cannot achieve in this life, the only person who can stop you, is yourself. Be as open and transparent as you call out the cravings of your soul and be as specific as you possibly can. Then, have a look over your list and prioritize the order into the most important to the least. This way you will not get overwhelmed with all your brilliant ideas.

Take it step by step, and *write down an action plan to support these goals* in reaching their full potential.

We need to speak fluidly and confidently to the Universe when it comes to manifesting our desires, or otherwise we will receive mismatched vibrational frequencies.

The action plan may involve requesting spirit for help, and if so, commit yourself to being open to the signs. Have faith that what you want will come to you, but be flexible and place no expectations, for the Universe may have an even better outcome destined for you!

Once you are clear on your goals, enter a deep meditation to engrave your wishes upon the new moon. To close the circle, recite the following New Moon Prayer and thank the Universe for its love and dedication. And so it is.

# New Moon

As I welcome this new moon,
I look deep within myself.
I reflect over the life I have led
and the life that I wish to lead.
In my sacred space
I embark upon new beginnings
and I listen to my Eternal Soul
as to what it is that I truly desire.
On this day, grant me the
courage to pursue my dreams.
Bless me with your harmony
to ignite the pathway to my greatest success.
I wish for peace, happiness, and health
to everyone around me.
And for the abundance of love
that surrounds us to be received by all.

Phoebe Garnsworthy

# Full Moon

I harness the energy of this Full Moon and
ask for your blessings to fulfill my dreams.
I feel your loving vibrations move through
my heart and into this sacred space
providing me with the wisdom, guidance
and skills necessary to overcome any
challenges in my life.
I release my past pain and welcome change
with a curious mind and open heart.
I know that my hard work has not gone
unnoticed and that rewards will be received
in accordance to the Divine time.
Thank you, La Luna, my Love.

Phoebe Garnsworthy

# Full Moon Prayer

The full moon brings forth an opportunity to fulfill your dreams, symbolizing the completion of the cycle that has been. Do not be discouraged if your manifestations have yet to surface into fruition, have faith that the Universe is still preparing your wishes and that you will be gifted with greater rewards than you could have possibly imagined.

The most important element of the full moon is the energy that it brings. Many feel a surplus of vibrations circulating within their body, a strong need to move creatively or act upon their goals. Every day from the birth of the new moon to the full moon, we have been gaining our strength and wisdom to receive our wishes. When the moon has reached its full potential, you too will embody similar emotions. Perhaps you will feel a strong calling to live your life in a certain way or embark upon ideas that have been simmering in your mind. Trust your intuition and act upon these desires! This is your time to shine!

The full moon influences our energetic pull of creativity within us, weaving our dream of destiny into full swing, it is during this time that it is important to illuminate all the blessings in your life with blissful gratitude.

Open your sacred space (ideally with direct vision of the full moon), and allow yourself to 'moon bathe' during your meditation. Call upon the energies of Grandfather Sun and Grandmother Moon to commence your ritual.

*Journaling Questions:*
*What am I grateful for today?*
*What am I proud of myself for today?*

List all the wonderful areas of your life that you are grateful for (remember, the more gratitude you express, the more that will come to you) and follow with a list of what you are proud of yourself for.

Utilize the surplus of energy from full moon by surrendering yourself into the present moment, allowing anything that no longer serves you to be released.
This will open up the space for new energy to grow and bless your life.

Close your circle with a meditation and reciting your full moon blessing from the page before. And so it is.

# Your Invitation for Higher Vibrations

In every moment of every day you are offered an invitation to harness higher vibrational energy using the power of your voice, thoughts and feelings.

Every word has their own particular level of sound energy. The more positive a word is, the higher the frequency, and the more negative a word is will result in a lower vibrational frequency.

These sound energies attach themselves to us, so it's important to be mindful of the words you are speaking and thinking as well as the words that belong to other people who your surround yourself with.

Negative words exist as part of the shadow self, and although it is not particularly pleasant to relate to these frequencies, they too are a part of us, and we need to honor both the dark and
light that exists in our world.

If you find yourself speaking, feeling or embodying negative vibrations, first accept that it exists and then ask what can be learned from its presence (if anything). Once you have observed without judgement, make a conscious choice to let that vibration go, and welcome in beautiful, loving light energy.

You can release energy through various forms of exercises, dance, singing and meditation. Once released, focus on cleansing your space (internally and externally), and then replenish your soul using the harmonious vibrations of the universe around you. Other ways to invite in positivity is through experiences with others - sharing laughter with a friend, or offering help to another in need with no conditions for something to be given in return.

Check your own vibrational levels using the words on the following page. Do this by reciting each word and feeling how you resonate with it. When speaking the negative words make an effort to let them go (exhale noisily), and when reciting the positive words, invite that beautiful energy in using deep inhalations.

*Journaling Questions:*
*On a scale of 0-10 what is my vibration today?*
*Why is this? What did I do, or not do that has influenced the above answer?*
*What can I do to raise my vibration higher?*
*What people, places or things, give me high vibrations and low vibrations?*

# Today, I let go of:

- ◆ Fear
- ◉ Guilt
- ◆ Worry
- ◉ Anger
- ◆ Regret
- ◉ Expectations
- ◆ Limiting Beliefs
- ◉ Negative Thoughts
- ◆ Things I can't Control

*Phoebe Garnsworthy*

# Today, I Welcome:

- ◆ Love
- ✺ Change
- ◆ Gratitude
- ✺ Happiness
- ◆ Healing Energy
- ✺ High Vibrations
- ◆ Strong Boundaries
- ✺ A Healthy Lifestyle
- ◆ Putting Myself First
- ✺ Positive Affirmations

*Phoebe Garnsworthy*

# Sacred Smudging Prayer

I call upon the energies of Spirit to cleanse this space with me.

May you guide me as we remove any negative energy that lies here.

With this smoke I release anything that no longer serves me and

I invite healing, loving light energy to enter this space.

Grace me with your presence and bring forth positive vibrations

to love, nurture and bless all who enter here.

Thank you.

*Phoebe Garnsworthy*

*\*Please ensure all windows are open before smudging.*
*Never leave the flame unattended and be cautious of smudging near*
*children, the elderly or those with sensitive respiratory systems.*

# Sacred Smudging Prayer

Just as we need to cleanse and replenish our energy internally, it's important to cleanse the energetic space around us too.

This is achieved by smudging dried plants and herbs. To do this, let the edge catch alight of your chosen dried leaves, and then blow the flame out, allowing you to work with the smoke to enter your space and remove any impure vibrations. This is an ancient technique passed down from the earliest civilizations and can be found in every country around the world. Two wonderful plants to use for this are white sage, and palo santo.

**White sage** is commonly used as it scientifically proven to remove harmful bacteria from the air as well as any potent energy that is lingering in your energy field.

**Palo Santo** is known for it's healing vibrations and positive tranquility. The scent of Palo Santo opens up your creative power and harnesses confidence as you ignite with your Higher Self.
Before commencing your sacred smudging prayer, ensure your space is clean and tidy. Then, follow the steps below:

**Step One** - Open up all windows and doors to ensure the smoke is able to exit the room easily. Do not to burn the smoke around elderly people, children or those who have breathing difficulties.

**Step Two** - Bundle dried leaves and herbs and tie them together with natural string or cotton (not flammable). Get a small dry dish that will not trap the heat (and burn your hard) and can easily be used to extinguish the bundle if necessary.

**Step Three** - Commence your sacred space ritual as you wish. Take a few deep breaths and visualize the intention for your smudging session.

**Step Four** - Carefully light your bundle on fire and then blow it out quickly. Read the following Sacred Smudging Prayer to support your energy cleansing ritual.

*Journaling Questions:*
*Write down how you feel before and after you smudged your space. Note down emotions and feelings from within and also of your space. Feel the energy of the room and remember to cleanse your space as often as you feel you need to.*

# Today's Affirmation

We use affirmations to honor the divine soul within us, and raise our vibration to connect to our Higher Self and bring forth the infinite wisdom that surrounds us. When we weave affirmations into our self-love and self-care routine, we encourage self-empowerment and self-fulfillment, enabling us to handle anything that comes our way with patience, understanding and gratitude.

Affirmations are powerful statements that connect the conscious and unconscious mind with a goal to positively influence our thought pattern, behavior or habits. It supports the belief that we create our own reality, we are the architects of our future and that we hold the greatest wisdom that there is to be known about our life.

Affirmations work by influencing our thought patterns from negative to positive. When we focus our attention on the positives in our life we in turn attract more positive vibrations, falling upon the belief that like energy attracts like energy.

When we clear our mind of anything that holds us back from living in alignment with our Higher Self, we are able to focus solely on the positives that surround us, and the blessings that we are manifesting.

To harness the power of affirmations recite the statement clearly and repeatedly, allowing the vibrational frequency of your mind and body to truly embody and feel that energy. Upon doing so, you will naturally shift into a higher realm to support the truth of this statement. The more we speak positive truths about ourselves, the more we believe it and the stronger our innerpeace becomes.

When creating your own affirmations ensure to speak confidently and to use terminology that implies that you are living this statement in this present moment as though it is already done.

Look over the suggested list of positive affirmations, take what resonates with you, add to it, and let it go.

*Journaling Questions:*
*What are my favorite affirmations?*
*Where in my life do I need extra support?*
*What limiting belief do I hold about myself that I would like to change?*
*What affirmation could I create that supports the above?*

# Affirmation:

I am in alignment with my Higher Self.

I welcome challenges with ease as I go about my day.

I release all that no longer serves me

and I open the space for something new to enter my life.

I know that I am divinely looked after by the Universe at all times.

I am a beautiful soul within a magnificent body.

I have the courage, confidence and ability to achieve my dreams.

I am perfect, exactly as I am.

I have all the answers I need right now.

I am enough.

*Phoebe Garnsworthy*

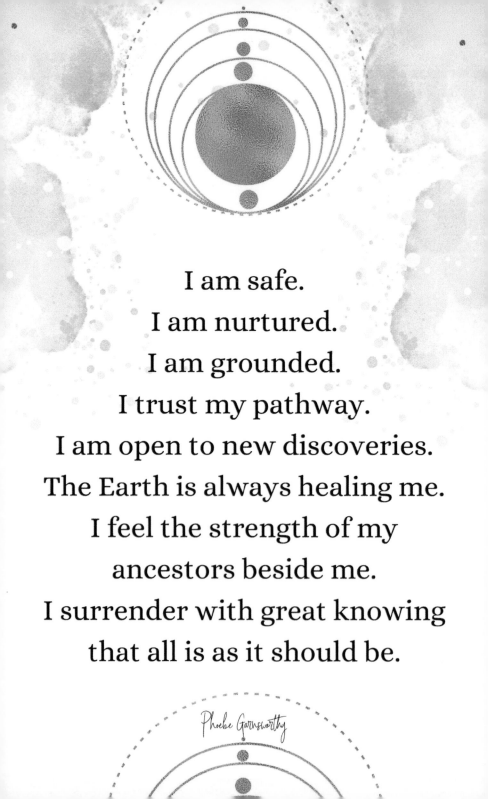

I am safe.
I am nurtured.
I am grounded.
I trust my pathway.
I am open to new discoveries.
The Earth is always healing me.
I feel the strength of my
ancestors beside me.
I surrender with great knowing
that all is as it should be.

*Phoebe Garnsworthy*

# Grounding Affirmations

When we are grounded we feel safe, nurtured and supported. From this space we can make decisions confidently and have complete clarity over our life. When we are ungrounded we may feel depressed or anxious, we may have difficulty making plans or find ourselves indecisive or dependent on unhealthy habits.

It's easy to ground ourselves, the tricky part is recognizing that we are ungrounded as the symptoms may cross over many other areas of confusion.

The simplest way to balance our energy and ground ourselves is by getting out into nature. Spending time amidst grass, trees, and feeling the energy of life around you. But not always can we get into nature immediately, and so we can achieve the feeling of being grounded using a combination of creative visualization and grounding affirmations. Imagine a cord of radiant energy connecting you to the core of the Earth, feel this energy support of mother nature and repeat your grounding affirmations.

*Journaling Questions:*
*What does being grounded mean to me?*
*What are my favorite ways to ground myself?*

# Confidence Affirmations

Whatever we speak about ourselves has the power to become real. Whatever you deem yourself worthy of will manifest before your very eyes. What area of your life do you wish to feel more confident in? And most importantly, what are you doing to support this confidence to build from within?

Consistent acts of self-love and self-care will bring forth confidence in any area of your life that you wish. If you wish for confidence in your unique beauty, face or body - speak love notes to yourself in the mirror, decorate your life with positive self-talk, and participate in heavenly indulgences that promote happiness from within. If you desire confidence in your talents or intelligence, keep moving your vibration toward experiences that encourage growth of your abilities. The more you practice, the better you become and the more natural this confidence will evolve into your life.

You are the divine creator of your world and the way you choose to live your life is completely up to you.

*Journaling Questions:*
*Where in my life am I lacking confidence?*
*What activities can I introduce into my life consistently to build my own inner strength?*
*How can I measure this success?*

I am worthy of love, of peace and of happiness.
I am worthy of success, of miracles and magic.
I have endless talents within me
that I choose to nurture.
And these gifts are what make me
unique and beautiful.
I listen to the cravings of my soul
through the voice of my intuition.
I nurture my passions with confidence and ease.
In this sacred space, I know that anything is possible.
For I am the creator of my life,
I am the architect of my future.
Whatever I dream can be manifested,
whatever I believe I am worthy of
can become real.

*Phoebe Garnsworthy*

# 7 Chakra Affirmations -

I am connected to the energies of the Universe

I listen to my intuition with ease

I speak authentically my truth

I love myself unconditionally

I am confident and resilient

I am sensual and creative

My Soul is grounded and nurtured

Phoebe Garnsworthy

# 7 Chakra Affirmations

The 7 chakras are believed to be the 7 energy portals in your body that balance the health of your mental, spiritual and physical self.

These portals are spinning energy, both absorbing and expelling, with the sole purpose to harmonize the flow of energy amidst your physical, mental and emotional self. If you are happy and at peace with your life your chakras will turn fluidly and with ease. If they are spinning slowly, they are under-active or if they are spinning too fast, they are considered overactive.

There are various ways to harmonize your chakras, and speaking words of affirmations is one of them. It's also important to use visualization while doing so. To do this, imagine the color of the chosen chakra as a light energy, entering the space where the portal resides.
Use your breath to breathe positive energy into this space and exhale to release anything stagnant that is withholding the chakra from performing at its ultimate best.

You can also do movements or drawing exercises to channel that particular chakra, release energy and rejuvenate its power. As you read the list below tune in and see if any of the descriptions resonate with you at this time. Take note of the chakra and brainstorm some creative ways to focus on healing that energy portal. Use your own intuition as you self-reflect over your life and discover how you can heal your current challenges. Create some positive habits and notice how you feel from doing the work to clear and harmonize your energetic chakras.

**Root Chakra** is the color red and located at the base of your spine. It is the closest to the earth and for this reason connects to grounding, security, survival and your health. It is the foundation for all the other chakras. When this chakra is overactive you will feel a sense of loss with self usually in the form of anxiety (your security and survival is threatened). If it is under-active you will be more displaced with your security, distant and daydreaming (depressive thoughts), unable to hold reality.

**Sacral Chakra** is located just above the root chakra, in the lower abdomen. It is connected to your creativity and sexuality. It is the color orange. Addiction and obesity is a trait of an overactive sacral chakra, and a lack of sex drive or inability to create or a lack of passion is the result of an under-active sacral chakra.

**Solar Plexus Chakra** is located just below the belly button and is connected to our power and confidence.

It is the color yellow. Digestive issues and uncontrollable emotions are generally the results of an overactive solar plexus chakra. Lack of confidence and fatigue is a symptom of a under-active solar plexus chakra.

**Heart Chakra** is in your heart center and is the color green. It is connected to love and compassion. Lack of self-love, loss of boundaries and unhealthy choices are the results of an overactive chakra. Loneliness and body image issues are a trait of an under-active heart chakra.

**Throat Chakra** is the color blue and sits in your neck. It is connected to your communication channel and supports the truth in your words. Someone who is outspoken with little self-awareness holds an overactive throat chakra. And someone who is shy, or timid when voicing their opinion is the result of an under-active throat chakra.

**Third Eye Chakra** sits just between your eyebrows, on your forehead. It is your intuition channel with your soul. It is the color indigo. When a third-eye chakra is overactive the person tends to call upon the spirit world in extreme such as tarot card readings or a desire for paranormal experiences. When someone has an under-active third eye they have difficulty tuning into their own intuition and they are closed off from the spiritual synchronicities that surround them.

**Crown Chakra** is the color violet or white and it hovers just above the top of your head. It is the connection with the spirit world in the cosmos above. An inability to control your energy, headaches and a disconnection with your physical self is the result of an overactive crown chakra. Depression and inability to meditate is a result of an under-active crown chakra.

As you read the following 7 chakra affirmations, recall the area that it relates to. Start at the bottom of the page and work your way up. Feel the weight of each affirmation as it cleanses and realigns your charkas. Be sure to meditate before and/or after as you visualize loving light energy within and around you to heal your mind, body and soul.

When our chakras are aligned and the energy is flowing organically, we are able to live in alignment with our Higher Self. From this space we can make confident life choices, and heed the wisdom needed to live a truly fulfilled and blessed life.

*Journaling Questions:*
*From the list above, which chakra feels out of balance and needs work on? What is an activity that I could do to help heal this chakra?*

I open my heart and listen to my Higher Self
as I am guided with love.

*Phoebe Garnsworthy*

PHOEBEGARNSWORTHY.COM

# Phoebe Garnsworthy

## about the author

Phoebe Garnsworthy is an Australian female author who seeks to discover magic in everyday life.
She travels between the worlds of the seen and unseen, gathering ancient wisdom and angelic energy. Her writings reflect a dance with the mystical and wonderful, an intoxicating love potion to devour in a world that overflows with forgotten love and enchantment.

The intention of her writing is to encourage conscious living and unconditional love.

**www.PhoebeGarnsworthy.com**